Borderline

THE MUSINGS OF A BROKEN MIND.

Amber-Louise Diskin

BookLeaf Publishing

Borderline © 2021 Amber-Louise Diskin

All rights reserved.

No part of this publication may be reproduced, stored in a retrieval system, or transmitted, in any form or by any means, electronic, mechanical, photocopying, recording or otherwise, without the prior written permission of the presenters.

Amber-Louise Diskin asserts the moral right to be identified as author of this work.

Presentation by *BookLeaf Publishing*

Web: www.bookleafpub.com

E-mail: info@bookleafpub.com

First edition 2021

To those who may be broken or lost.

Acknowledgement

Mum & Dad, for pushing me to pursue my dreams.

John, for promising to back me in the past, the present and the future.

Preface

You should be warned, in advance, that topics written here may be triggering and upsetting.

1. Dad

Yesterday you said goodbye to me,
Your eyes brimming with tears,
Staring at the blank hospital ceiling,
Apologising for the previous years.

Yesterday I held my mother,
Her eyes soaking my shirt,
Terrified to leave you,
Your absence is what hurt.

Today I promised I'd see you again,
Not knowing you'd last the night,
I told you I loved you with all my heart,
Everything was going to be alright.

Today you defied deaths order,
And beat him out the door,
Heart still pumping
life throughout,
Your strength is
evermore.

Tomorrow I will return,
I'll prove how much I care,
The truth I write to you,
A thousand kisses could not prepare.

2. Anger

This isn't fear,
The cascade of tears,
The burning makes me cry harder,
Fuelling this pit of lava,
Bubbling in my gut,
Stuck in a rut,
This ticking timebomb about to erupt,
The guilt, the pain, the sadness,
My recipe of disaster,
It answers no master,
Bordering on madness.

3. Not Alone

You found me,
When all I wanted was silence,
You found me,
In need of absolute guidance.

You found me,
When I craved a routine,
You found me,
And made me feel seen.

You found me,
Drowning myself in liquid sorrow,
You found me,
Promising a better tomorrow.

You loved me,
Connected by our string of fate,
You loved me,
With your ability to wait.

You loved me,
Through all of my pain,
You loved me,

When there was nothing to gain.

You loved me,
And became my best friend,
You loved me,
Promising it would never end.

I love you,
Regardless of distance,
I love you,
My heart full of persistence.

I love you,
You're all I require,
I love you,
No matter what may transpire.

I love you,
Through all of the dark,
I love you,
Promising never to
disembark.

We have each other,
Through the good and
the bad,

We have each other,
When life makes us sad.

We have each other,
With matching smiles,
We have each other,
No matter the miles.

We have each other,
We don't care wherever,
We have each other,
Promising to be forever.

4. Gone

Piercing daggers through skin,
Blood washing away all traces of sin,
A stained now red sleeve rolls down,
All smiles back off to allow a frown,
Trying to end a useless life,
Stabbing herself with a crimson knife.

A wave of pain lets the prisoners escape,
The daring patterns taking shape,
Tears of excruciating pain,
Loneliness is enough to send you insane,
Her final breath feels so cold and frail,
It leaves her body, she's ever so pale.

5. Machine

We are cogs in a machine,
Wasted and unclean,
You boast your immunity,
In an ocean of inopportunity.

Hoping to escape,
My plans begin to take shape,
Building my potential,
The steps I take are sequential,

Continuing to resist them,
Breaking free of the system,
No end in sight,
I will stand and fight,

For a future I witness,
This is all just business,
Hard work turns the wheel,
Despite how we feel,

Unable to cope,
For stable futures we hope.

6. Prisoner

A prisoner to my brain,
Chest throbbing with pain,
Hands dripping with sweat,
Clearly upset,
Mouth dry as sand,
I cannot stand,
Legs getting weak,
Unable to speak,
Alone in my cell,
My personal hell,
A lifelong sentence,
No chance of repentance.

7. Split

My racing thoughts,
A collection of fears,
Trying to grasp sense,
Through waves of tears,
My splitting mind,
Fractured over the years,
The only solace,
Found after many beers,
Disappointment attacks,
Stabbed by sharp spears,
Never quite fitting in,
Different from my peers,
My mood is monotone,
Shifting between two gears.

8. Hell

Hell is the way you scheme,
Mid-dream,
For just 5 more minutes,
As you drift back asleep,
Hell is my unkempt hair,
Try not to swear,
No matter how hard I try,
A lions mane that cannot be tamed,
Hell is pulling tights over fat thighs,
Having to improvise,
To hide the tears on the inside,
From too much tugging,
Hell is the lump in your throat,
Don't choke,
From unchecked dates,
Pouring fermented cream in coffee.
Hell is watching the clock,
Tick-tock,
The countdown to lunch,
Waiting for food to
arrive,
Hell is the daily
routine,
It's obscene,

A continuous grind,
Crushing my spirit to dust.

9. Dreamcatcher

With your twine wrapped circles,
And feathered tails,
Your intricate webs and beads,
Catching my nightmares,
As a spider catches prey,
Trapping bad tales,
Fearsome monsters,
In your woven net.

10. Lonely

Locked in my cell,
Of flesh and bone,
Knees pulled tightly to my breast.

A yearning deep,
A guttural groan,
Fighting with the demon in my chest.

The need and begging,
To not be alone,
A constant fearful test.

11. Darkness

A broken window,
Shards of glass,
Pierce my skin,
Pain will pass.

A cold chill,
Runs through my spine,
A tremble in my body,
Detonating a land mine.

A flickering light,
Cast a shadow,
Alone in the dark,
Fear will overthrow.

12. Touch

I pretend not to care when you touch me,
Uncomfortable at first,
Your touch is the worst,
Dealing with this curse,
Trying to avoid your attention.

I pretend not to care when you touch me,
Deflecting your gaze,
Counting the days,
Until you stop your ways,
Inside I'm dying even more,

I pretend not to care when you touch me,
Comments on my clothes,
Your obsession shows,
I am the victim you chose,
Hoping someone will save me.

I pretend not to care when you touch me,
You make my skin crawl,
I feel so small,
Pressed into the wall,
I pretend not to care though,
Especially, when you

touch me.

13. "Friend"

I locked myself away,
To deal with your fight,
I promised I would stay,
Everything would be alright.

I put myself second,
Let myself hurt,
Every time you beckoned,
My problems in the dirt.

You told me I wasn't there,
Wasn't a good friend to you,
You didn't seem to care,
That your words were far untrue.

For years I would endure,
The ignorance you gave,
My heart nothing but pure,
I was just your emotional slave.

Buried in the earth,
I suffered for a while,
Searching for my
worth,

A reason for me to smile.

Now I've shed my skin,
I can worry about myself,
You were never truly kin,
I removed you from that shelf.

Now you've gone and lost me,
I decided to be smart,
You were only going to disagree,
It was time for me to depart.

14. Survive

Define me by my fight,
For I will never give in,
Punch the air from my lungs,
I will breathe again.

Cut my porcelain skin,
My scars show my strength,
Break my brittle bones,
They will heal at length.

I will never stop,
Combatting the motions,
Survival is my goal,
Ignoring the notions.

15. Home

Home is where you are,
Safely tucked under your arm,
Even when the distance is far,
You protect me from harm.

Home is your voice,
Like syrup on breakfast,
You are always my choice,
A meal I hope will last.

Home is how you smell,
Spicy and sweet at the same time,
A refuge in this scape of hell,
The ladder I hope to climb.

Home is the beat of your heart,
Thrumming deep in your veins,
The string of fate will never part,
Upon my soul your love stains.

16. Adventure

Black words on ivory pages,
Being chased by evil mages,
Caped crusaders with wards in tow,
Assassins with sharp knives they throw,
Masked figures in shadows hide,
Protagonists full of pride,
Hunting monsters in the dark,
Antagonists leave their mark,
Bookshelves act like shrines,
Escaping between the lines,
Increasingly difficult to leave,
These tales that I weave,
Finding love where none dare look,
I live my life within a book.

17. Anxiety Attack

The room is spinning,
Upon an axis of its own,
Delirium is settling,
Words are just noise
Confusion is hitting,
Lost to the world,
Panic is rising,
Judgement is cast,
Legs are bouncing,
Holes burning my flesh,
Body is falling,
F
  A
    L
      L
        I
          N
            G
                D
                  O
                    W
                      N

18. Fear

Electricity jolts my body,
Keeling over and clutching my stomach,
As my chest begins to constrict,
Airways feeling blocked,
Suffocating on my thoughts,
Forgetting how to breathe,
Lost in the darkness,
Another day.

19. Brain

My mind is like a sieve some days,
All information slips through the gaps,
My memory not serving its purpose.

My mind can be an enemy,
Voices collapsing walls, breaking doors,
Abusing me with endless torture.

My mind can be a weapon,
Cutting deep with every word,
Fighting back, against the world.

My mind can be brilliant
Excellence and creativity comes to light,
Like magic, pen to paper, a spell.

My mind can be a friend,
Shielding me from all the pain,
Always by my side.

My mind can be an escape,
Daydreaming,

remembering,
Silent.

20. Alien

When she closes her eyes she frowns,
The world disappears,
The mind of a troubled child,
Helpless and in fear.

Familiar streets turned foreign,
Lost in a land called home,
Stumbling past blank faces,
Forever cursed to be alone.

She no longer believes in herself,
No longer wants to live,
Her heart has been drowned,
Hope shredded to pieces.

Printed in Great Britain
by Amazon